What Are You Making?

Written by Alison Hawes
Photographed by Antony Elworthy

Collins

Here's what we need:

laundry basket

ping pong balls

rubbish bin

pen

funnel

shredded paper

feather boa

cardboard

crepe paper

egg carton

aluminium foil

2

feather dusters

What are you making?

I'm making the body.

What is she making?

She's making the head.

What is he making?

He's making the eyes.

What are they making?

They're making the claws and teeth.

What have you made?

We've made a monster!

What are you making?

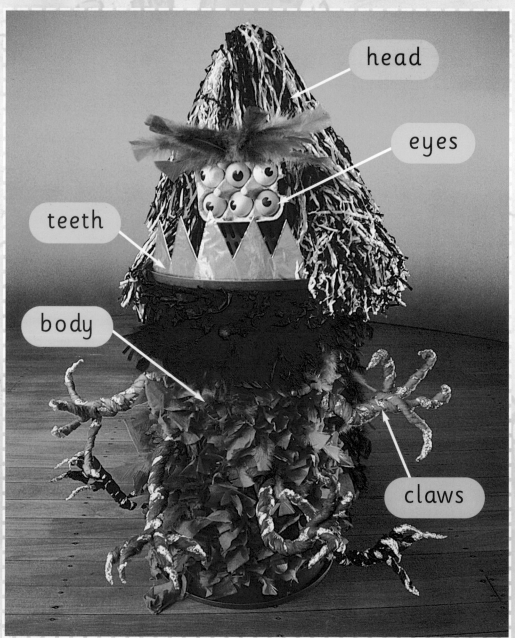

head

eyes

teeth

body

claws

body

head

eyes

claws

teeth

🐾 Ideas for guided reading 🐾

Learning objectives: make predictions from a brief look at covers, including blurb, title; recognise the main elements that shape texts; use syntax and context when reading for meaning; distinguish fiction and non-fiction texts; read more challenging texts which can be decoded using acquired phonic knowledge and skills; take turns to speak, listen to other's suggestions

Curriculum links: Knowledge and Understanding of the World; Build and construct, selecting appropriate resources; Look closely at similarities, differences, patterns and change; Physical Development: Handle malleable materials safely and with increasing control; Creative Development:

Explore texture, shape and form in two or three dimensions; Use imagination in imaginative play; Express and communicate ideas, thoughts and feelings by designing and making

High frequency words: are, have, he, is, she, we, what, you

Interest words: ping pong balls, rubbish bin, laundry basket, pen, funnel, shredded paper, feather boa, cardboard, crepe paper, egg carton, aluminium foil, feather dusters

Resources: scrap materials, paper, pencils, whiteboard

Word count: 46

Getting started

- Ask the children what they like making and what sort of materials they use.

- Look at the front cover together. Ask them to name the materials and items.

- Write the names of the items (e.g. *egg box, shredded paper, feather duster*) on a whiteboard with the children. Re-read the words together, noting the phonic cues that help (*initial sounds, blending the phonemes*).

- Ask the children to discuss in pairs what they think the children are going to make. Ask pairs to share ideas with the whole group.

Reading and responding

- Read the title page together. Notice the question mark and re-read the title together with expression.